90p

This book belongs to

P. M. Dangerfield.

...llege House, 45, East Street, Faversham, Kent.
Faversham 2302. November 3rd 1981

GREAT GRANDMOTHER GOOSE

This is —— ——'s book.
If it be lost, and you it find,
I pray you heartily, be so kind
As to take a little pain
To send me home my book again.

GREAT GRANDMOTHER GOOSE

◆

Helen Cooper

◆

Illustrated by

Krystyna Turska

HAMISH HAMILTON

First published in Great Britain 1978 by
Hamish Hamilton Children's Books Ltd
90 Great Russell Street, London WC1B 3PT
ISBN 0 241 89550 2
Printed in Great Britain by
Cox & Wyman Ltd,
London, Fakenham and Reading

FOR KATY AND ANNE

Introduction

In the days before printing was invented, when books were written not on paper but on parchment made from the skins from the vast flocks of sheep that the book-hungry monasteries maintained around themselves, and when every word of the Bible or a romance or a school textbook had to be written out by hand, then men were very careful about what they took the trouble to preserve in the precious medium of the written word. Nobody thought it worth the effort and expense to record mere children's rhymes, and besides, why write down what everybody knew? Even now, in the age of printing, any four-year-old can recite "Hey diddle diddle" without the benefit of literacy, and any mother can sing "Rock-a-bye, baby" without having to look up the words. So we do not know what songs and rhymes were sung to children in the Middle Ages; but we can be certain that mothers did sing to their babies, that children did have their own rhymes and catches, that nurses repeated moral tags with that extra dimension of imagination that can turn a truism into "Jack Sprat".

This book is an attempt to bring together some mediaeval poems that might have filled the place now taken by nursery rhymes. They come from all kinds of places: scribbled in the margins or on the flyleaves of manuscripts, from commonplace books or minstrels' anthologies, even from church walls. They are set down by sermon-writers and chroniclers in the course of their work, by scribes and clerks in moments of relaxation. Some are moral, some practical, some personal and vindictive; some are dance-songs, some are political slogans, some are charms. They cover, in fact, the same kind of range as the nursery rhymes known today. They may not have been written specifically for children, but neither were many of our own rhymes; what matters is that children might have heard them sung," enjoyed them and recited them in turn. The poems we know as nursery rhymes began to be recorded in significant numbers only from the early seventeenth century, in songbooks and as broadside ballads, and it was another hundred years after that before the first collection was printed that could be called a book of nursery rhymes. The poems I have collected here are their ancestors.

The main problem in making an anthology of this kind is the imbalance in the poetry that has been preserved. Songs that were commonplace in oral tradition were unlikely ever to be written down, and it is only rare chance that has preserved a few fragments. If poetry was going to be recorded at all, then the expensive commodities of parchment and a scribe's time were likely to be spent on weightier verse; the mediaeval secular lyrics that have come down to us are outnumbered three or four to one by religious poems, and the number of surviving rhymes that can be proved to have been popular or traditional is minute. Sometimes a secular poem can be sensed behind a religious re-working, but only the refrain survives intact; for instance, we have several mediaeval religious "lullabies", but only their "lully, lullay" refrains to suggest the songs that underlie them. Moreover, the only verse we possess, not itself a lullaby, that we know was sung by mothers as they rocked the cradle, is hardly the the sort of thing we would consider suitable for children, besides being too fragmentary, as it has survived, to stand alone as a nursery rhyme. There are, none the less, many poems that have that distinctive quality of imaginative range, of the fantastic or grotesque, the hauntingly beautiful or equally hauntingly trivial, that characterizes all nursery rhymes; and these are the ones I have gathered together here.

In date they all come from the Middle Ages or shortly after; the most recent were recorded in the sixteenth century, but all of these were probably already traditional by then. The oldest is the earliest mediaeval lyric to survive, composed when the language was just beginning its progress from Old to Middle English. A bare handful have come down to us as modern nursery rhymes. The collection ends as our own nursery rhymes begin.

The rhymes are meant to be read to, or by, children, so I have not included every poem that might have qualified—"Thirty days hath September" has an ancient lineage but is already completely familiar; schoolboy conundrums depending on the finer points of Latin grammar would be out of place. Where translation or substantial editing was necessary, I have tried to keep faithful to whatever quality of the original poem first caught my imagination; usually this was compatible with literal accuracy, but I have occasionally adapted or abridged the rhymes. Significant departures from the originals are recorded in the notes, where readers will also be able to find out about the places the poems come from and some of the things they talk about.

Animals and Other Things

The cricket and the grasshopper went out to fight,
With helmet and habergeon all ready dight;
The flea bare the banner as a doughty knight,
The beetle trumpeted with all his might.

The hare sat upon the hill and fastened her shoon,
And swore by the buttons that were thereupon
That she would not rise nor be gone
Till she saw twenty hounds and one.

The miller sat upon the hill top,
And all the hens of the town came up.
The miller said, "Shoo, hens, shoo!
I will not shake my bag for you."

I have twelve oxen, and they be fair and brown,
And they go a-grazing down by the town.
With hey, with ho, with hoy!
Saw you not mine oxen, you little pretty boy?

I have twelve oxen, and they be fair and white,
And they go a-grazing down by the dyke.
With hey, with ho, with hoy!
Saw you not mine oxen, you little pretty boy?

I have twelve oxen, and they be fair and black,
And they go a-grazing down by the lake.
With hey, with ho, with hoy!
Saw you not mine oxen, you little pretty boy?

I have twelve oxen, and they be fair and red,
And they go a-grazing down by the mead.
With hey, with ho, with hoy!
Saw you not mine oxen, you little pretty boy?

The hare went to market scarlet for to sell,
The greyhound stood before him the money for to tell.

At my house I have a jay
Who knows what all the animals say.
He can bark like a fox,
He can low like an ox,
He can hiss like a goose,
He can bray like an ass,
He can croak like a frog,
He can growl like a dog,
He can chatter like a wren,
He can cackle like a hen,
He can neigh like a steed;
Then he's ready for his feed.

Clym, clam
The cat leapt over the dam.

My dame hath in a hutch at home
A little dog
With a clog.
   Hey, dog, hey!

A white horse up the hill,
A black horse down the hill,
A grey horse for a gravelled way,
And for every road, a bay.

If your horse has four white feet,
Give him to your foe;
And if he has three,
Do even so.
If he has two,
Give him to your friend,
But if he has just one,
Keep him till the end.

The false fox came unto our farm,
And meant to do our geese some harm.
  With how, fox, how! with hey, fox, hey!
  Come no more unto our house to bear our geese away!

The false fox came unto our coop,
And there he made our geese to stoop.
  With how, fox, how! with hey, fox, hey!
  Come no more unto our house to bear our geese away!

He took a goose fast by the neck,
And then the goose began to quack.
  With how, fox, how! with hey, fox, hey!
  Come no more unto our house to bear our geese away!

The goodwife came out in her smock,
And threw her distaff at the fox.
  With how, fox, how! with hey, fox, hey!
  Come no more unto our house to bear our geese away!

The goodman came out with his flail,
And smote the fox upon the tail.
  With how, fox, how! with hey, fox, hey!
  Come no more unto our house to bear our geese away!

He threw a goose upon his back,
And then he went forth with his pack.
  With how, fox, how! with hey, fox, hey!
  Come no more unto our house to bear our geese away!

The false fox went into his den,
And there he made full merry then.
  With how, fox, how! with hey, fox, hey!
  Come no more unto our house to bear our geese away!

The goodman said unto his wife,
"The false fox liveth a merry life."
  With how, fox, how! with hey, fox, hey!
  Come no more unto our house to bear our geese away!

“**P**eace be with you!” said the fox,
“For I am come to town.”

It fell upon the next night,
The fox came up with all his might,
Without coal or candlelight,
When he came to the town.

“Peace be with you!” said the fox,
“For I am come to town.”

When he came all in the yard,
Sorely were the geese a-feared;
"Some of you shall take it hard
Before I go from town!

"Peace be with you!" said the fox,
"For I am come to town."

He seized a goose in the blink of an eye;
Fast the goose began to cry!
Out ran the men as they might hie,
Saying, "False fox, lay it down!"

"Peace be with you!" said the fox,
"For I am come to town."

"Nay," he said, "that may not be –
She shall go unto the wood with me;
She and I beneath a tree,
Among the berries brown.

"Peace be with you!" said the fox,
"For I am come to town."

"I have a wife, and she lies ill;
Many small whelps she has as well.
They shall surely eat their fill
Before they lay them down.

"Peace be with you!" said the fox,
"For I am come to town."

The wren loves to run
Where the millstones turn,
But she doesn't care a jot
For the fiddle or the flute.

Stroke owl
  and shape owl
    and ever is owl
      owl.

The white dove sat on the castle wall,
I bent my bow and made her fall,
I put her in my glove, both feathers and all.

I have a gentle cock,
  Crows me in the day;
He makes me rise early
  My matins for to say.

I have a gentle cock,
  Come of kindred great;
His comb is of red coral,
  His tail is of jet.

I have a gentle cock,
  Very nobly bred;
His tail is of purple,
  His comb of coral red.

His legs are of azure,
  So slender and genteel;
His spurs are of silver white
  Up to the heel.

His eyes are of crystal
  Locked all in amber;
And every night he perches him
  In my lady's chamber.

The lion is wonderfully strong,
and full of wiles of woe.
And whether he play,
or take his prey,
he'll kill you, would he or no.

Be careful of a playful bear, just in case he bites!
He seldom finishes his game unless he bites or smites.

I will you all swallow, like it or not.
Though some I will save, and some I will not.

Sir Penny

Penny is a hardy knight,
Penny is mickle of might,
Penny of wrong he maketh right
  In every land where he may go.

If I have pence both good and fine,
Men will ask me out to dine;
"All that I have shall be thine" –
  Certainly they will say so.

And when I have none in my purse,
Penny better nor penny worse,
Then they do not care a curse:
  "He was a man, let him go!"

Money, money, now hay good day!
money, where hast thou be?
Money, money, thou goest away,
and wilt not bide with me.

He that spends much and gets nothing,
And owes much and has nothing,
And looks in his purse and finds nothing,
He may be sorry and say nothing.

He that loveth well to fare,
Ever to spend and never spare,
Without the gold to make it good,
His hair will grow right through his hood.

Jolly fellow, jolly,
Jolly fellow, jolly,
If thou have but little money
Spend it not in folly,
But spend it on a pretty wench,
And she shall help thee at a pinch.
Hey, jolly fellow, jolly.

How Things Are . . .

The man that at Christmas
  has a dog look after the larder,
And then in March
  puts a sow in charge of the garden,
And in May makes a fool
  hear a wise man's counsel,
He shall never have good larder,
  fair garden,
    nor well-kept counsel.

Two women in one house,
Two cats and one mouse,
Two dogs and one bone,
    May never agree in one.

I had my goods and my friend;
I lent my goods to my friend;
I asked my goods of my friend;
I lost my goods and my friend.

The hart loves the wood, the hare loves the hill,
The knight loves his sword, the woodman loves his bill,
The fool loves his folly, the wise man loves his skill,
And what a shrewish woman loves is to have her will.

Peace maketh plenty,
Plenty maketh pride,
Pride maketh plea,
Plea maketh poverty,
Poverty maketh peace.

Bring the ox to the table,
He'll want to go back to the
stable.

It stands written in a book,
He that has no horse must go on foot.

The mouse goes abroad
When the cat is not lord.

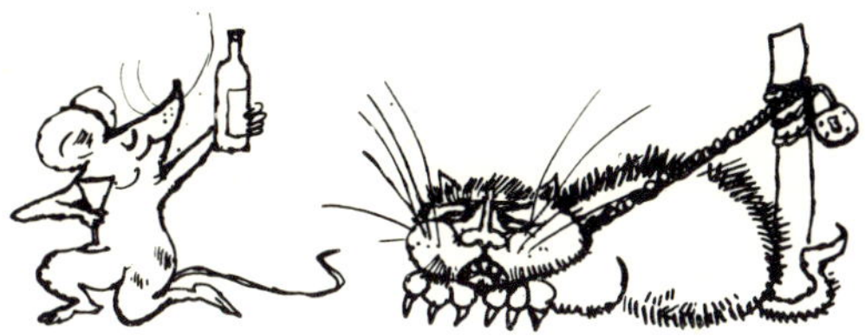

John, John, pick a bone,
Tomorrow thou shalt pick none.

The cat can well pick
Whose beard is best to lick.

The cat will fish eat,
But she will not wet her feet.

Keep well ten
And flee from seven,
Rule well five
And come to heaven.

He that will in Eastcheap eat a goose so fat
With harp, pipe and song,
He must sleep in Newgate lying on a mat,
Be the night never so long.

Lo, fool, how the day's sped!
Cast folly now to the cock.
Trouble is waiting ahead;
It is almost twelve of the clock.

Our Lord commanded
  that flax should increase,
The wether bear wool
  and the sheep its fleece.
If you stood naked
  as the skin of a stone,
However fair your body
  then you would wish for some.

Whoever builds his house all of sallows,
And spurs his blind horse over the fallows,
And lets his wife seek saints and hallows,
Is worthy to be hanged on the gallows.

January	By this fire I warm my hands;
February	And with my spade I delve my lands.
March	Here I set my seeds to spring;
April	And here I hear the birds sing.
May	I am light as bird in the tree-top;
June	And I take pains to weed my crop.
July	With my scythe my mead I mow;
August	And here I shear my corn full low.
September	With my flail I earn my bread;
October	And here I sow my wheat so red.
November	At Martinmas I kill my swine;
December	And at Christmas I drink red wine.

. . . and How Things Aren't

When sparrows build churches and steeples high,
    And wrens carry sacks to the mill,
And mice mow corn with waving their tails,
    And seagulls bring butter to the market to sell,
    And goslings ride hunting the wolf to kill,
And flounders run with spears in armour to defence –
    Then shall no man to other do offence.

As many toads as breed in Ireland,
As many griffins as breed in England,
As many cuckoos as sing in January,
And nightingales as sing in February,
And as many whales as swim in the fen,
So many be there in cities of good men.

When Adam delved and Eve span,
Who was then the gentleman?

Take a miller that will not steal,
And a weaver that measures well,
And a priest that is not greedy,
And lay beside them a dead body,
Through the virtue those three have,
The dead corpse shall come alive.

You will never, fast or slow,
Make an eagle of a crow,
Nor make a falcon of a buzzard,
Nor hardy knight make of a coward.

All Sorts of People

As King Canute rowed past Ely,
The monks within sang merrily.
"Row nearer land, knights!" said the King,
"And let us hear how these monks sing."

A friar, a hayward and a polecat sat on a bench,
A tapster sat beside their thirst for to quench.
  Which was the worst of the company?
  Knaves the lot of them, say I!

Tom-a-lin and his wife and his wife's mother,
They went over a bridge all three together.
The bridge was broken and they fell in.
The devil go with all, said Tom-a-lin.

Harry Hotspur has a halt,
  And he is fallen lame.
Francis Physician for that fault
  Swears he was not to blame.

Baker, baker, belamy,
Be careful of the pillory.
Unless you make good bread,
Somebody will have your head.

Philip Sedgebarrow,
You've neither plough nor harrow,
You lack both bow and arrow.
You are a sorry marrow!

Terlee terlo, terlee terlo,
  Tertee terlee terlo!
Jolly shepherd sat upon a hill,
So loud he blew his little horn
And kept his flock right well,
    Early in a morning,
    Late in an evening,
And ever blew this little boy
  So merrily piping:
    Tirraly terlo!

Maiden in the moor lay,
  in the moor lay –
Seven nights full, seven nights full.
Maiden in the moor lay,
  in the moor lay –
Seven nights full and a day.

Well was her meat.
  What was her meat?
The primrose and the violet.

Well was her drink.
  What was her drink?
The cold water of the well-spring.

Well was her bower.
  What was her bower?
The red rose and the lily flower.

Maiden in the moor lay,
  in the moor lay –
Seven nights full, seven nights full.
Maiden in the moor lay,
  in the moor lay –
Seven nights full and a day.

In and Out of Love

I have a young sister
far beyond the sea,
Many be the love-gifts
she sent to me.

She sent me the cherry
without any stone,
and so she did the dove
without any bone.

She sent me the briar
without any bark,
She bade me love my lover
with no pain at heart.

How should any cherry
be without stone?
And how should any dove
be without bone?

How should any briar
be without bark?
How should I love my lover
with no pain at heart?

When the cherry was a flower,
then it had no stone.
When the dove was an egg,
then it had no bone.

When the briar was a seed,
then it had no bark.
When the maiden has that she loves,
she has no pain at heart.

"**H**ey trolly lolly lo,
Maid, whither go you?"
"I go to the meadow
To milk my cow."

"Then at the meadow
I shall you meet,
To gather the flowers
Both fair and sweet."

"Nay, God forbid,
That may not be,
Indeed, my mother
Then shall us see.

Nay, in good faith,
I will not go with you;
I pray you, Sir,
Let me go milk my cow."

Come over the bourn, Bessy,
  My little pretty Bessy,
Come over the bourn, Bessy, to me.

There was a maid came out of Kent,
  Dainty love, dainty love,
There was a maid came out of Kent,
    Dangerous be.
There was a maid came out of Kent,
Proper and fair to compliment
As any maid that ever went,
  For so should it be.

Tell me, wight in the broom,
How I should behave me
To make my husband love me.

Hold your tongue still,
And have all your will.

We shall make a jolly castle
High beside the river's brim.
No man shall come therein
If he cannot swim,
Unless he has a boat of love
To go a-sailing in.

I chose my lover at stone-casting,
And I lost him at wrestling.
  Alas, that he so soon fell!
  Why couldn't he stand better, the fool?

Doh, doh, the nightingale sings a merry song.
I care no longer for thy love, for I have loved too long.

Words of Power

Saint George, Our Lady's knight,
He walked by day, he walked by night,
Till he found the witch of the night;
And when he had found her
He beat her and he bound her,
Till truly there her troth she plight
That she would not come by night
Within seven acres' space of land
Where Saint George was ever named.

Ship by the sea flood,
Be thy days good!

Ship by the sea brink,
May no water thee sink!

Come wind, come rain,
Come he never again!

Fire and water, wind and land,
I would have under my hand.

Any man that meets a hare,
He shall never the better fare
Unless he lay down on the land
Whatever he carries in his hand –
Be it staff, be it bough –

And bless him with his elbow;
And with well good devotion
He shall say an orison
In the worship of the hare:
Then may he well fare.

The hare, the scotart,
The go-by-ditch, the momelart,
The steal-away, the fern-sitter,
The evil-met, the grass-biter,
The friendless, the woodcat,
The late-at-home, the broomcat,

The white-belly, the furzecat,
The wild thing, the leaper,
The wind-swift, the lurker,
The lightfoot, the dew-hopper,
The go-by-ground, the west-looker,
The deer with the leather horns,
The beast that liveth in the corn,
The beast that every creature scorns,
The beast no man dare name.

When you have said this through,
The hare's power is laid full low;
Then you may journey forth,
East and west and south and north.
Have now good day, Sir Hare!
May you so well fare
That I meet you by and by
Either jugged or in a pie.

Running, Dancing, and Standing Still

How many leagues to Beverley?
– Eight, eight and other eight.
Think you I shall get thither tonight?
– Yes, if your horse be good and light.

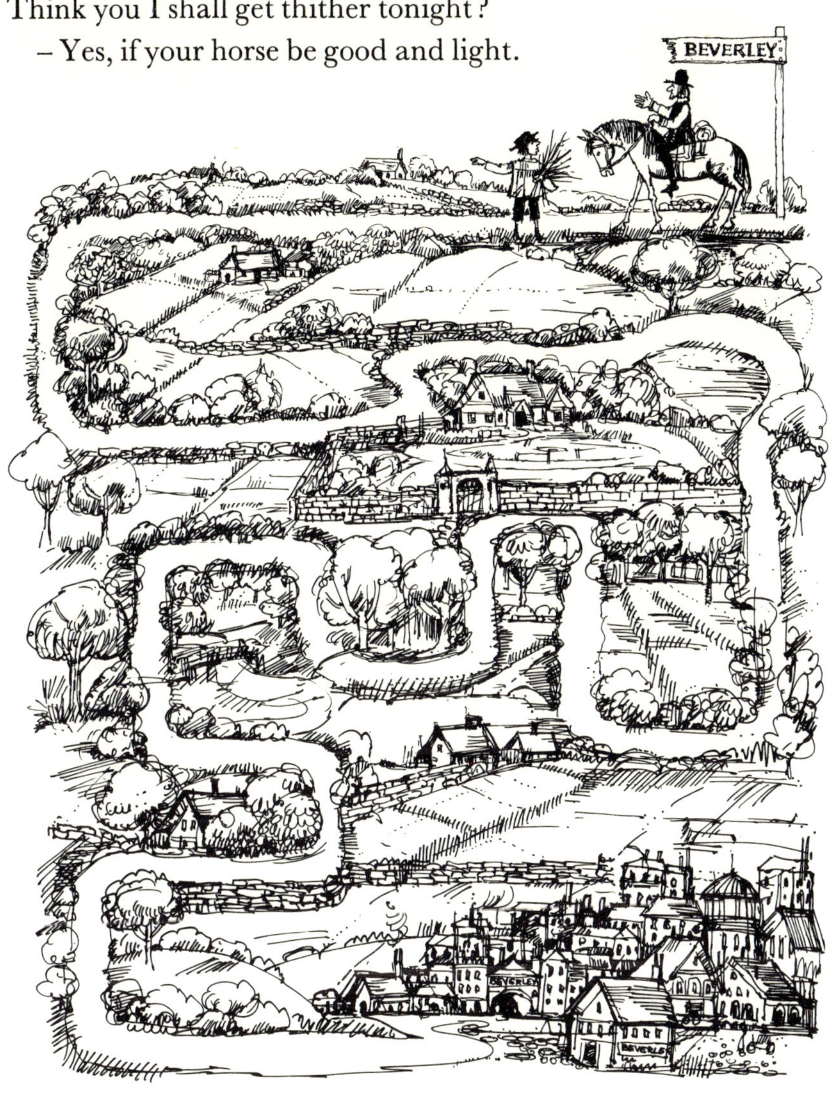

Ha, ha, petty-pace,
I am still
Where I was!

I am of Ireland,
and of the holy land
of Ireland.

Good sir, pray I thee,
for Saint Charity,
come and dance with me
in Ireland.

I am of Ireland,
and of the holy land
of Ireland.

Hop, hop, Willikin, hop, Willikin!
England is mine and thine.

Stand all still,
    Still, still, still,
Stand all still,

Still as any stone.
Trip a little with thy foot,
And let thy body go!

Everything and Nothing

Keep an eye ever turned to the wood.
Up on the hill the lame buck stood.
Two and three make how many?
Three half pence come to one penny.

I saw an ape thatching a barn,
And a frog wind balls of yarn,
And a codfish sowing corn.

I saw a hedgehog cut and sew,
And a worm a whistle blow,
And a kipper bend a bow.

I saw a pudding eat a pie,
And a sow hang out her washing to dry.
It isn't long since I told a lie!

There was a man that had nought.
Thieves came and robbed him, and took nought.
He ran out, and cried not.
Why should he cry? He lost nought.
  Here is a tale of right nought.

As I lay on a bundle of straw
   Cuddling of my cow,
There came along to me Jack Daw,
   And said, "Neighbour, how now!"

Our dame milked the mare's tail.
   When our maid came by
The cat was licking the milking-pail,
   So she popped her in a pie.

A cow had stolen a calf away
   And put it in a sack.
Forsooth, I sell no puddings today.
   Masters, what do you lack?

Robin is gone to Huntingdon
  To buy our goose a flail.
Little Spip, my youngest son,
  Was hunting of a snail.

Our maid John was here tomorrow;
  I don't know where she's gone.
Our cat lies sick and feels great sorrow.
  And there's an end of my song.

When pucket's away,
Then shall we go play.

When the pucket is asleep,
Then may we sow our wheat.

Mock has lost her shoe;
Now what is she to do?

I shall take to wash down in the town
Clothes that were black and clothes that were brown.

Hale and ho, rumbelow,
Stir well the good ship and let the wind blow!

Here comes the Prior of Prickingham with his Convent.
Unless you keep the order well, you'll quickly repent!

Hale and ho, rumbelow,
Stir well the good ship and let the wind blow!

My heart of gold as true as steel,
  As I leaned on a staff,
In faith unless you love me well,
  Lord, how did Robin laugh!

My lady went to Canterbury
  To offer up her prayers;
She met with Kate of Malmesbury.
  Why water an apple-tree with tears?

Nine mile to Michaelmas
  Our dame began to brew;
Michael set his mare to grass;
  Lord, how fast it snew!

Your gown, my love, is furred with blue;
  Sleep, and the cock will crow.
Against the wind his horn he blew.
  To the water goes the crow.

There's plenty more to tell, indeed:
  The cat lies in the cradle;
The goose to the green has made good speed;
  A penny for a ladle.

Tirlery lorpin, the laverock sang,
  So merrily pipes the sparrow,
The cow broke loose, the rope ran home.
  Sir, God give you good morrow!

Holly and ivy had a great quarrel,
Who should have the mastery
  In lands where they go.

Then spake holly: "I am fresh and jolly;
I will have the mastery
  In lands where we go."

Then spake ivy: "I am loud and proud,
And I will have the mastery
  In lands where we go."

Then spake holly, and kneeled on his knee:
"I pray thee, gentle ivy, say nothing ill of me
  In lands where we go."

Little pretty nightingale
Among the branches green,
Give us of your Christmas ale
In honour of St. Stephen.

Robin Redbreast with his notes
Singing in the choir
Warns you all to get warm coats,
For winter's drawing near.

My bridle's lying on the shelf;
If you will have any more,
Be so kind as to sing it yourself,
For here you have all my store.

Notes

The notes are an attempt to pick out points of interest in the rhymes, and to summarize what is known about their origins. Wherever possible, I have taken the texts direct from manuscripts or early printed sources; but as too many manuscript shelf-marks look decidedly offputting, I shall introduce the reader to just a few of the great sources of mediaeval verse. For anybody who wants to study the originals, I give the reference number for each poem in the *Index of Middle English Verse* (edited by Carleton Brown and Rossell Hope Robbins, New York 1943, and its *Supplement*, 1965), where a full list of manuscripts and publications containing the rhyme can be found. The rhymes without *Index* numbers are either recorded too late, or are excerpts from longer poems, or have only been discovered in the last few years, and for those I give more specific details. For those who would like to get more idea of the poetic context of the rhymes, Rossell Hope Robbins' *Secular Lyrics of the XIVth and XVth Centuries* (revised edition, Oxford 1955) is the inevitable sourcebook, and I give page references for the rhymes to be found there. Alternatively there are two more recent anthologies, of wider scope, which may be more easily available: *Medieval English Lyrics* edited by R. T. Davies (London 1963), and *Middle English Lyrics* edited by Maxwell S. Luria and Richard L. Hoffman (New York 1974).

This is —— ——'s book A bookplate verse used in two manuscripts, one from the fifteenth century and one from the sixteenth. A more strongly worded verse of the same period runs:

This book is one thing,
  Christ's curse is another.
He that stealeth the one,
  May God send him the other.

(*Index* 1417.5.)

The cricket and the grasshopper Each verse of this poem is followed in the manuscript by a Latin translation; it was inscribed at the end of a grammar book late in the fifteenth century. A "habergeon" is a mail-coat. (*Index* 3324; Robbins p. 104.)

I have twelve oxen From Richard Hill's Commonplace Book (Balliol College, Oxford, MS 354), a collection of romances, lyrics, legal notes, records of the births of his seven children, and so on, made by a citizen of London in the early sixteenth century; the poems of this kind that he records were presumably already traditional—certainly several are known from much earlier. (*Index* 1314; Robbins p. 42. See also pp. 26, 33, 39, 40, 74.)

The hare went to market One of a number of paired English and Latin tags in a fifteenth-century manuscript in the Bodleian Library. "Scarlet" was a kind of rich cloth rather than just a colour. (*Index* 3372.5. See also pp. 33, 59.)

At my house This poem, and a few others, were inserted into a kind of grammatical miscellany, presumably a school textbook, in the late fifteenth century. It accompanies a Latin version, which was presumably designed as an aid to vocabulary. I have rationalized the last line from a puzzling original. (*Index* 430.8.)

Clym, clam This couplet is one of a number of English tags and verse fragments included in Nicolas Bozon's *Contes Moralisés*, a collection of tales made in the fourteenth century. Most of the work is in French, but Bozon himself was probably an Englishman writing for a bilingual English audience—at this period French was still the language of culture, and usually the medium of education even when what was being taught was Latin. *Stroke owl* (p. 18) is from the same source. (*Index* 635.5.)

My dame hath in a hutch The sixteenth-century Cambridge don Gabriel Harvey scribbled this rhyme and *When pucket's away* (p. 78) on the flyleaf of one of his books, now in the Old Library, Magdalene College, Cambridge.

It is also recorded in Thomas Ravenscroft's *Pammelia*, a songbook of largely traditional songs published in 1609, which includes such items as an early version of *Ding, dong, bell.*

A white horse and *If your horse* Sayings and jingles on the properties of horses are still widely known; one strikingly close to the second was still current a hundred years ago. These two are from a fifteenth-century collection of recipes, medicines and such things. (Bodleian MS Wood empt. 18; see Rachel Hands, Medium Ævum 41 (1972) p. 237.)

The false fox This poem is an interloper in a fifteenth-century religious anthology. I have shortened it slightly. (*Index* 3328; Robbins p. 44.)

"*Peace be with you!*" Fifteenth century; written on a blank leaf before the flyleaf at the end of a manuscript of drearily moral French works. (*Index* 1622; Robbins p. 43.)

The wren loves to run This poem is inserted into three manuscripts of a verse treatise written by Walter of Bibbesworth in the late thirteenth century to teach French vocabulary to English children. The word I translate as "millstones" is "schowe" according to one reading of the original—presumably the "shoe" of the mill, the receptacle that channels the grain from the hopper to the "eye" of the runner-stone. An alternative reading is "scholke", meaning a group of sheaves. (*Index* 1851.)

Stroke owl From Bozon's *Contes Moralisés*, along with *Clym, clam*. "Shape" is MS "schrape", probably "scrape"—more grotesque but less visually suggestive. (*Index* 3218.5.)

The white dove W. Wager's morality play *The Longer Thou Livest, The More Fool Thou Art* was written in the 1560's but contains a number of traditional songs. This is one of them; others are *Tom-a-lin* (p. 45), *There was a maid* (p. 53) and *Little pretty nightingale* (p. 83).

I have a gentle cock Chaucer's Chauntecleer, in the Nun's Priest's Tale, also has a comb redder than coral, azure legs and white "nayles", but it is his bill, not his tail, that is jet-black. This poem comes from an insignificant-looking pocket-book-sized paper manuscript of the fifteenth century, British Library MS Sloane 2593, which is one of the principal anthologies of mediaeval English lyrics. It may have been a minstrel's personal collection. There is more than one way of reading this poem, but that is also true of *Goosey, goosey gander.* (*Index* 1299; Robbins p. 41. See also pp. 25, 57.)

The lion The sentiment expressed in this poem is at odds with the official mediaeval lore on lions, which describes them as sparing the prostrate, women and children "unless they are very hungry". This poem and the two following accompany Latin versions in a collection of otherwise almost entirely moral and religious pieces. (*Index* 3353.)

Be careful of a playful bear The bear is presumably the dancing or baiting sort—wild bears had become extinct in England before the Norman Conquest. Dancing bears were a common form of entertainment in the Middle Ages, and to judge from manuscript illuminations on the subject they were very seldom muzzled; so the rhyme may have a more practical application than one might think. (For origin, see note above; *Index* 3353.)

The Dragon The speaker is identified in Latin in the manuscript—"from the dragon's mouth". Unselective consumption is not a usual characteristic of dragons, so far as I know; and though the dragon was also a symbol of the Devil, the theology would hardly be orthodox in this rhyme. It is as well to take it on its own terms, and the nursery-rhyme category seems to fit it best. (For origin, see *The Lion* above; *Index* 3353.)

Penny is a hardy knight The unreliability of money is a widespread theme in mediaeval literature of all kinds. I particularly like the idea of Sir Penny as a knight-errant who rides about wronging rights. Abbreviated from Sloane MS 2593 (see *I have a gentle cock*). (*Index* 2747; Robbins p. 50.)

Money, money The burden of a long carol (i.e. a song with stanzas and a repeated refrain, originally used as a dance-song with a solo singer and the dancers as chorus), from the fifteenth century. (*Index* 113.)

He that spends much Recorded in three manuscripts, including Richard Hill's Commonplace Book; two contain a second stanza. (*Index* 1163; Robbins p. 81.)

He that loveth well This verse used to be inscribed on the wall of the dining hall at Launceston Priory, Cornwall, above the table where the personal servants of the guests would sit (see R. H. Robbins, *Archiv* 200 (1963–4) p. 342). It is also recorded in a mid-fifteenth century manuscript. (*Index* 1156.)

Jolly fellow, jolly The burden of a carol from the anthology entitled *XX Songes* printed by Wynkyn de Worde in 1530. (*Index* 87.5.)

The man that at Christmas When the printer of the work known as *The Book of St. Alban's* (1486) had finished setting up in type the section devoted to hunting, he found he had some spare pages before the treatise on heraldry which was to follow; and this poem is among the items he used to fill up the space—others are *Two women* (p. 31) and *Whoever builds his house all of sallows* (p. 34). It is also found in an earlier manuscript. (*Index* 4106.)

Two women in one house A proverb recorded several times in the fifteenth century, including the *Book of St. Alban's* (see *The man that at Christmas*). (*Index* 3818.)

I had my goods A widely recorded proverb; some versions substitute "silver" for "goods". (*Index* 1297; Robbins p. 81.)

The hart loves the wood This poem is the first item in a late fifteenth-century commonplace book from Broome Hall, Norfolk, best known for the *Abraham and Isaac* play it contains. The rhyme next surfaces, in a pithier form, in the seventeenth century, and it is still known today. (*Index* 3372.6.)

Peace maketh plenty A widely recorded fifteenth-century proverb. (*Index* 2742; Robbins p. 81.)

Bring the ox to the table Mid-fifteenth century. (*Index* 548.8.)

It stands written A couplet preserved in the comic-moral *Dialogue of Solomon and Marcolphus*, printed in 1492. (*Index* 1640.3; see also p. 33.)

The mouse goes abroad From Richard Hill's Commonplace Book. Cat-and-mouse proverbs and tales were widely known in the Middle Ages; the most famous is probably Langland's fable of belling the cat in *Piers Plowman*. (*Index* 3438.6.)

John, John A tag with an accompanying Latin translation, from the same manuscript as *The hare went to market*. (*Index* 1793.9.)

The cat can well pick This proverb, widespread in the later Middle Ages, is first recorded in the early fourteenth century. There is a different rhyming version in *Solomon and Marcolphus*; other versions usually do not rhyme. Two manuscripts give differing Latin equivalents. (*Index* 3318.6.)

The cat will fish eat A widespread proverb found in unrhymed versions from the early fourteenth century; the rhyme I give here is from *Solomon and Marcolphus* (see *It stands written*). (*Index* 3318.8.)

Keep well ten The references are, of course, to the ten commandments, the seven deadly sins and the five wits. The proverb is found in Richard Hill's Commonplace Book and a number of other earlier manuscripts. (*Index* 1817; Robbins p. 80.)

He that will in Eastcheap "According to Aristotle"—or so the manuscript says. Eastcheap was the area where the cooks' shops were concentrated; Newgate was a prison from early in the Middle Ages. (*Index* 1172.5.)

Lo, fool These lines were scratched on the wall of Barrington Church, Cambridgeshire. It is probably a doomsday poem. (*Index* 1925.)

Our Lord commanded This little poem is one of the oldest in this collection, probably from the early thirteenth century. It is written in the margin of a collection of moral and religious pieces from the library of Corpus Christi College, Oxford. (*Index* 4238.)

Whoever builds his house Chaucer makes the Wife of Bath's latest husband quote these lines at her, but she refuses to take any notice of his "old saw" and sets off on a pilgrimage all the same—"hallows" are shrines. The proverb was widely known, and the *Book of St. Alban's* is among the other sources for it. (*Index* 4101.)

By this fire Labours of the months similar to these are illustrated time and again in mediaeval calendars, often very beautifully; unfortunately both the manuscripts that contain this rhyme have very poor illustrations. (*Index* 579.)

When sparrows build churches This is an abbreviated version of a satirical poem on women; consumer tests suggested that the original moral was incomprehensible. From Richard Hill's Commonplace Book and other manuscripts. (*Index* 3999; Robbins p. 103.)

As many toads This jingle looks like an ancestor of "as many red herrings as grow in the wood". It occurs in the course of Alexander Barclay's eclogues (very early sixteenth century). Barclay is working from a Latin model, but in many places in his work he seems to catch the rhythms of folk rhymes and proverbs, and this is one of the most striking.

When Adam delved A political theme has never been a bar to a nursery rhyme. This proverb is best known for its use as a slogan in the Peasants' Revolt of 1381, but it is probably older than that. It is recorded earlier in Latin, but it seems likely that the original was in English. It was a common tag throughout the fifteenth century, and versions are also found in Germany and the Low Countries. Richard Hill is one of those who record it. (*Index* 3922.)

Take a miller This rhyme is found in the Maitland MS in the Pepys Library, Magdalene College, Cambridge, which also contains many poems by Dunbar and other Scottish poets. Millers were notoriously dishonest (Chaucer's Reeve's Tale is a wonderful instance of the theme). Langland and other social critics refer to the sharp practices of weavers in stretching the selvedge of the cloth, and the rapaciousness of priests must be one of the commonest themes of all mediaeval writings. (*Index* 3248.5.)

You will never, fast or slow This version of the proverb comes from the fourteenth-century romance of *King Alisaunder*. The original birds of the second line were the goshawk and the kite.

As King Canute rowed past Ely Thomas of Ely tells us in his Chronicle that Canute (reigned 1017–35) composed this song when he was travelling to Ely by water—the easiest way to get there before the seventeenth-century draining of the Fens. Thomas says that people were still singing and dancing to the rhyme in his own time, some hundred and fifty years after Canute's visit. The story could be true; but whether the poem dates from the eleventh century or the twelfth, it is still the oldest in this collection, and the earliest recorded Middle English lyric. This is how it looks in the original:

> Murie sungen the munaches binnen Ely
> Tha Cnut ching reu ther by.
> Roweth cnites noer the lant
> And here we thes munaches saeng.

It makes a very good action song for a baby or a small child. (*Index* 2164.)

A friar, a hayward and a polecat A doggerel rhyme (originally a couplet) distantly reminiscent of "the butcher, the baker, the candlestick-maker". Friars were the object of vituperation throughout the later Middle Ages; a fifteenth-century proverb compares them unfavourably to foxes. The hayward acted as the overseer of work in the fields, and also as a kind of village policeman. From a sixteenth-century commonplace book. (*Index* 35.5.)

Tom-a-lin From Wager's *The Longer Thou Livest* (see the note on *The white dove sat on the castle wall*), but probably also referred to in *The Complaint of Scotland*. This is one of the oldest nursery rhymes to have come down to us in an only slightly altered form.

Harry Hotspur has a halt Henry Percy, nicknamed Harry Hotspur, the rebel against Henry IV, caught his contemporaries' imagination as he did Shakespeare's; this rhyme makes it sound as if it was a name to conjure with even on the nonsense level. It occurs at the end of a metrical life of St. Cuthbert. (*Index* 1185.)

Baker, baker, belamy The pillory was the normal punishment for a baker who sold underweight or adulterated loaves; the threat of retribution is a warning of the Virgin's wrath in the original. "Belamy" is from the French "bel ami", "fair friend". The rhyme is tucked away among a collection of Latin saints' lives and miracles. (*Index* 459.)

Philip Sedgebarrow An early fourteenth-century scribe rounds off his copy of a long Latin poem dealing with the main events of the Old and New Testaments with this rhyme, which just fills up the remaining lines on the page. Alongside it is a grotesque kind of dragon with a human face who appears to be speaking the verse—or possibly eating it, or even vomiting it up. "Marrow" means "fellow"—a sense in which it survived until recently in dialect. The rhyme has not previously been published in full, so I give it here:

Phelip seggebarwe
thou nast plow ne harwe
the fayllez bowe and arue
thou art a sory marwe.

(Bodleian MS Auct. F 5 16 p. 131, *Index* 2752.)

Terlee terlo This poem was traditional in England and Scotland by the late sixteenth century, and there are a couple of possible earlier Scottish references to it, one in a list of old songs in *The Complaint of Scotland* (1549). The shepherd piping on his hill is one of the folk characters of the late Middle Ages. Little Boy Blue also has a horn to blow to his sheep, and so does the shepherd in the jingle in *King Lear* III.vi.

Maiden in the moor lay This is one of the Rawlinson lyrics, a dozen poems of the early fourteenth century written on a single leaf used in the binding of a later manuscript; the sheet shows signs of heavy wear and may have served as a minstrel's song-sheet. The song was widely known: sacred words are set to its tune (which has not survived) in the Red Book of Ossory (see the note on *Doh, doh, the nightingale*), and a preacher refers to it in the course of a sermon. In the manuscript the first half of the last line of the short stanzas is repeated twice before the full line is given, so that the verses are all of the same length; the repetition of the first verse is my own addition. There are two other Rawlinson lyrics in this collection, *I am of Ireland* and *Stand all still* (pp. 66, 68–9). (*Index* 3891; Robbins p. 12.)

I have a young sister The ancestor of some well-known folksongs. Fifteenth century, from Sloane MS 2593. (*Index* 1303; Robbins p. 40.)

Hey trolly lolly lo This is the earliest recorded version of the song on the wooing of a milkmaid, now widely current in folksongs and nursery rhymes ("Little maid, pretty maid, whither goest thou?"—"Down to the meadow to milk my cow"). *Hey trolly lolly lo* dates from the early sixteenth century, but this song or others like it must already have been traditional fifty years earlier when Sir Thomas Malory turned Sir Torre's mother into a milkmaid. Although it sounds like a folksong, this version is found in an elaborate manuscript of court music known as Henry VIII's MS. The full poem is quite long; I have used only the first stanza and the refrain. (*Index* 2034.5.)

Come over the bourn This refrain appears with a number of different sets of words from the fifteenth century onwards, but all the complete versions known to us are moral or political in theme and the original popular song that gave rise to them has been lost apart from these lines. (*Index* 3318.4.)

There was a maid From Wager's *The Longer Thou Livest* (see the note on *The white dove*).

Tell me, wight in the broom This is one of the older rhymes in the collection, from a thirteenth-century miscellany in Trinity College, Cambridge. Who was the wight in the broom? Perhaps it was a "wise woman" of the kind later harried as a witch (broom seems to have had some connection with witchcraft), or perhaps some kind of woodland oracle. In another manuscript, however, there is a little Latin story constructed around a similar English rhyme which gives a different explanation:

> A certain woman went to consult a fortune-teller about her husband, who knocked her about even though she didn't deserve it. The fortune-teller said to her, "I shall find you a remedy: fetch some wine, cheese and one shilling, go to the forest and put the things down, and say:
>
> Say, wight in the broom,
> What I am to do;
> I have the worst bond
> That is in any land."
>
> The fortune-teller, hidden in the brambles, replied:
>
> "If your bond is ill,
> Hold your tongue still."

(*Index* 3078.)

We shall make a jolly castle A popular song probably of the late fourteenth century, preserved in the course of a Latin sermon in a manuscript in Jesus College, Cambridge (13). The preacher goes on to compare the castle to the celestial city. (See Siegfried Wenzel, *Anglia* 92 (1974) p. 74.)

I chose my lover One of the oldest rhymes in the collection: the first two lines were used as a sermon text in the late twelfth century. A later manuscript gives the whole stanza. (*Index* 445; Robbins p. xxxix.)

Doh, doh, the nightingale Richard Lesdrede, a fourteenth-century bishop of Ossory, composed a number of Latin hymns to be sung to secular tunes. In his collection, the Red Book of Ossory, the first lines of the original English or Anglo-Norman popular songs are cited before each hymn; some, such as *Maiden in the moor lay*, are preserved in full elsewhere, but others, including this one, survive only here. The translation is slightly free. (*Index* 684.)

Saint George, Our Lady's knight An early fifteenth-century charm against the Night Mare. She was supposed to be a spirit monster that molested men and animals at night; the manuscript contains the further instruction, "Write this in a bill (on a piece of paper) and hang it in the horse's mane." (*Index* 2903; Robbins p. 61.)

Ship by the sea flood These gnomic lines are spoken by the young hero Horn to the boat that preserves himself and his twelve companions in the romance of *King Horn* (early thirteenth century).

Come wind, come rain From the manuscript of *The hare went to market.* (*Index* 644.5.)

Fire and water A request for power over the four elements (fire, air, water, earth) found in a number of manuscripts, including the one that records the Lion, the Bear and the Dragon. (*Index* 798.)

Any man that meets a hare That it is unlucky for a hare to cross your path is a very old superstition—this incantation for exorcising the bad luck goes back to the thirteenth century, where it is found in an anthology of mixed English and Anglo-Norman pieces. It is headed, "The names of a hare in English"; I have shortened the list by more than half. Fishermen at sea still sometimes think it unlucky to call a hare by its own name, and the same superstition was known in the mines.

"Scotart" is probably from "scot", an obsolete word for "hare"; "momelart" perhaps means something like "nibbler"; "west-looker" might be connected with the dialect "west" in the sense of "sty" (in the eye), so meaning "blear-eyed". (*Index* 3421.)

How many leagues to Beverley? This rhyme is preserved in a thirteenth-century sermon, where the preacher compares men who first hasten towards Heaven and then slacken their efforts to boys playing this game. The verse is given in Latin, the last three lines in English; the form of the verse I give here is from a seventeenth-century description of the game, with the mediaeval "leagues" substituted for "miles". The rhyme surfaces again as "How many miles to Babylon?" only in the nineteenth century. (*Index* 0.3.)

I am of Ireland Another of the Rawlinson lyrics (see *Maiden in the moor*). (*Index* 1008; Robbins p. 11.)

Hop, hop, Willikin This rhyme is said to have been sung in 1173 by Flemish mercenaries of the Earl of Leicester just before their defeat by the army of Henry II. It is recorded by the chronicler Matthew Paris in the mid-thirteenth century; it probably came to form part of a dancing-song. (*Index* 1252.)

Stand all still The last part of a drunkard's song found among the Rawlinson lyrics. (*Index* 4256.8; Robbins p. 106.)

Keep an eye ever turned to the wood A very early rhyme: the author of the Ancrene Riwle, a treatise written in the early thirteenth century to provide a rule of life for anchoresses (a kind of female hermit), uses the first line to warn his readers to remain spiritually alert. In copying out the treatise, the scribe of just one of the many surviving manuscripts of the Riwle accidentally completed the jingle. (*Index* 734.5.)

I saw an ape Adapted from a poem in Richard Hill's Commonplace Book. (*Index* 1350.)

There was a man From a fifteenth-century miscellany (*Index* 3546).

News, news, news, news! From an early sixteenth-century manuscript (*Index* 102.3).

When pucket's away A scribble by Gabriel Harvey accompanying *My dame hath in a hutch at home*, otherwise unknown.

Mock has lost her shoe John Skelton, writing in the early sixteenth century, describes these lines as "the end of an old song". We can only guess what the rest was like: perhaps it was on the lines of "Cock-a-doodle-doo, my dame hath lost her shoe". No form of that is recorded until a hundred years later, however, and then it was Peggy who had lost her shoe.

I shall take to wash From the same manuscript as *Tell me, wight in the broom* (*Index* 1389.5).

Hale and ho This is the only mediaeval sea-shanty that has come down to us. In a moment of boredom or rebellion, the clerk of the Tolsey Court

Book scribbled this in the middle of a list of the debts he was supposed to be recording. (Fifteenth century; see R. M. Wilson, *The Lost Literature of Medieval England* (1970) p. 178.)

My heart of gold as true as steel Slightly abbreviated from a mid-sixteenth-century anthology of festive poems entitled *Christmas Carolles.* Ravenscroft includes an even shorter version in one of his collections. (*Index* 2250.8.)

Holly and Ivy had a great quarrel One of a group of late fifteenth-century "holly and ivy" songs; the significance of the debate between them is now lost. It may have anthropological origins in the rivalry of male and female; by the late Middle Ages it may have been preserved in folk ritual or taken up as a courtly game, just as Richard II's court was divided between the supporters of the Flower and the Leaf. (*Index* 1225; Robbins p. 45.)

Little pretty nightingale From Wager's *The Longer Thou Livest.*